Adults with Autism

A Guide to Diagnosis, Inner-acceptance and Prosperity

© **Copyright 2018 - All rights reserved.**

The content contained within this book may not be reproduced, duplicated or transmitted without direct written permission from the author or the publisher.

Under no circumstances will any blame or legal responsibility be held against the publisher, or author, for any damages, reparation, or monetary loss due to the information contained within this book. Either directly or indirectly.

Legal Notice:

This book is copyright protected. This book is only for personal use. You cannot amend, distribute, sell, use, quote or paraphrase any part, or the content within this book, without the consent of the author or publisher.

Disclaimer Notice:

Please note the information contained within this document is for educational and entertainment purposes only. All effort has been executed to present accurate, up to date, and reliable, complete information. No warranties of any kind are declared or implied.

Readers acknowledge that the author is not engaging in the rendering of legal, financial, medical or professional advice. The content within this book has been derived from various sources. Please consult a licensed professional before attempting any techniques outlined in this book.

By reading this document, the reader agrees that under no circumstances are is the author responsible for any losses, direct or indirect, which are incurred as a result of the use of information contained within this document, including, but not limited to, —errors, omissions, or inaccuracies.

Table of Contents

Introduction

Chapter 1: Definition and Traits of Autism Spectrum Disorder

  Common Traits of ASD

  Genetic Issues

Chapter 2: Maybe I am Autistic, Now What?

Chapter 3: Rethinking and Realizing

  What does this have to do with ASD?

Chapter 4: The Process of Diagnosis

  Associated Psychiatric Issues

Meditation and Mindfulness

Chapter 5: Sharing Your Diagnosis With Friends and Family

Chapter 6: Self-Acceptance and Discovery

Sexual Issues

Concluding Thoughts

Introduction

I grew up having a very unique perspective of the world. Of course, I had no inclination or reason to believe that my perspective was unique. I just thought (took for granted, really) that everyone else saw things in the same way. We are all that way, and that is the reason we have misunderstandings and disagreements. After all, if we all saw things in the same way, nothing would ever be up for debate.

My first notion of disparity between perspectives was when I was 8 and my brother, who is a year younger, had a lot to say about a lot of things. I had no such urge, but it occurred to me that our perspective on what to say, when to say it, and how it was to be said, differed greatly.

I remember my parents commenting frequently – sometimes in front of my face, other times within earshot, of how silent I was and not as precocious as my younger brother. This was in the late seventies. When I related this to a friend recently, she said she felt bad for me, and I couldn't understand the reason for the empathy. My parents had merely stated a fact and they never meant it pejoratively. Being felt sorry for was more alien to me than being thought of as being silent. I was not silent, in fact far from it. There was a lot going on in my own head -the streams of data that were coming in from the observations and the thoughts of them kept me rather occupied. I never looked at anyone directly, only because I felt naked to do so. My world was in my eyes and letting someone see them felt too naked.

In 1998, my doctor suggested I take a simple test. Until then I didn't think I needed one, and frankly, I still don't think I need one, but here is the reason I submitted. As much as we know ourselves intimately from the inside, the picture is not complete until you know what it looks like from the outside. I merely took the test to understand myself better from the way the outside world in general may see me.

The test was straightforward and all I had to do was answer a number of questions honestly. I did.

I scored 38. That score is based on a simple test that is administered where you are asked about how you process certain events. They give you four possible answers to each question. In essence, the answers totally agree, somewhat agree, somewhat disagree or totally disagree. What I noticed about my answers was that they were all on one extreme or the other. Not one of those questions deserved a 'somewhat' response in my opinion. I mention this because it seems that one of the characteristics of ASD is that they tend to perceive things in black and white.

The test is scored on a scale from 0 to 60. Anything below 30 puts you in the non-Autistic category. Between 30 and 36.5 is supposed to mean that you have mild to moderate traits of ASD, and above 37 puts you in the severe category.

Before you start feeling bad for me, let me just say – don't. There is nothing to feel bad about. You being sad about me, or those similar to my condition, is like me being sad about you for not having some of the abilities I have. We are all different and just like autism is the general term for a spectrum of cognitive and emotional traits, being 'normal' is also a spectrum of cognitive and emotional traits. We are just different in those traits.

The only thing that is different is that there are more of you than there are more of us, so the number of one versus the other makes it look like there is something wrong with us. There isn't.

This book is designed to list out a number of things that people, both those within the spectrum, and those beyond, get to understand what it feels like to be in the mind of someone diagnosed to be within the Autism Spectrum Disorder (ASD).

Here is how I am going to lay it out for you over this book. Because it is my intention to keep it as simple as possible while being as detailed as I can, it is best that I frame each element on its own so that you can isolate its features and fine-tune it to alter the overall effects.

The first thing I suggest is that you do not embark on this endeavor to fix anything. Most people want to fix themselves to be 'normal' or the 'normal' folks want to fix us. I don't find it funny or sad. I find it is one of the reasons I'd rather keep to myself. Don't get me wrong, I still enjoy the company of others, but not in the way most people do. Each interaction with a person for me has to be intellectually stimulating, and the moment that stops, the utility of the time spent together has run its course. I then get up and leave. I am not rude. I am just honest.

The second thing is to understand that two factors are most important to those within the spectrum. The first is that the human mind is vast, but most people only develop it to be able to relate in binary fashion – this or that, yes or no, good or bad, vice or virtue. But life is more than that. There is no good or bad, right or wrong, sane or insane. It is all a matter of degrees, and if you can fathom that, you will find that you can understand your neighbor a lot better. I promised you two factors, so here is the second: each of us use two ways to define our place in this world. We use what we observe, and then we add that to what we think others observe when they see us. Slowly, in time, the two converge and make up part of our character and personality. If we feel that we are looked at poorly, we instinctually try to alter who we are to conform. Humans are social animals and the conformity gene is in all of us. The reverse is also true. We also tend to shun those who don't conform. That's when the problems start.

When I was a kid, we hardly heard the term autism. It was not prevalent in the parenting lexicon. We also didn't hear things like ADHD and other so-called abnormalities. That worked out to be a blessing because my parents didn't, for once, suspect I was different and so didn't treat me differently, and I had no pressure to conform or feel bad about myself. I grew up in a household that celebrated my strengths and patiently molded my weaknesses. That worked great for me and if it wasn't for the test I was asked to take, I would not have, for once, even guessed that I was autistic.

Chapter 1: Definition and Traits of Autism Spectrum Disorder

The first thing you need to keep in mind is that autism is not like having strep throat. You can't take antibiotics for it and be all better again in two days. It is not a specific condition, and not everyone manifests in the same way. It is a range of factors and a range of manifestations; that is because it is a state that defines your life by how it perceives the input.

Think of it this way. If you have good hearing, you get to speak really well as a child because all you have to do is mimic incoming sounds and you get it but, if you are deaf from the day you were born, then you will not have the ability to have anything to mimic. In the past, deaf children who did not speak were also misunderstood to be mute.

In the same way, deaf kids grow up to be mute as well, even though there is nothing wrong with their vocal cords. In the same way, most adults who are deemed to be different are not entirely different because of where they are on the autism spectrum, but rather it is because of the feedback loop that they were a part of as children.

The above consequence (of differentiated behavior) is only getting worse with time as the misunderstanding propagates unabated. As you read this book, are you surprised that someone on the severe side of the autism spectrum wrote it? If you are, you are not alone because most people are. The reason they are surprised can be synthesized down to two points.

The first reason they can't fathom it comes from the fact that the information that is out there is two-dimensional. Let me illustrate.

If you head to your favorite search engine and look for Autism Spectrum Disorder, you will find a string results that can be broken down as follows:

1. A brain disorder that:
2. Impacts how a person perceives the world around.
3. That results in an altered pattern of socialization, interaction and communication.

The points above are designed to be read as one sentence, but broken down so that you can see the different parts of the definition. First of all, it is taken for granted that this is a brain disorder and that automatically places a stigma on those who are diagnosed with it. Put a pin in that for a minute, as I will come back to that before this chapter is done.

Next, the definition talks about how it impacts perception. Now this is true. We perceive things very differently from those not diagnosed with ASD, but perception is not wholly a natural phenomenon in the human mind. It is only partially natural; the other part of it is nurtured. Perception is a function of nurture and nature, but the fact that we already started off by labeling it as a brain disorder, the finality of the matter is almost fait *accompli*. Once again, we will come back to this.

Then finally, we see that the expectation is diminished interaction, and communication results in an abnormal social pattern. What those who do not have ASD will tell you is all they can observe – they can't tell you what any one of us who are within the spectrum experience so, let me tell you what it is really like.

Part of my childhood was dominated by obsessive behavior. It is one of the symptoms of ASD, but doesn't happen in all of us. In me, it was fairly prevalent. I remember some of those incidences, but most of it is lost to time. There are a few my mom related to me, one in particular will serve as a good example here.

Around three years of age, my mom related that I developed a habit that I would walk around the house via specific paths. If a path from where I was to where I wanted to go was not established, I would connect the dots (so to speak). I would go to another point in the room and then get to my destination along a certain path. That slowly evolved, my mother continued, to a hub and spoke model, where wherever I was, I would walk along a specific path to the dining room (which was almost equidistant to other parts of the house and had an established path to every other point in the house) and then on to where my actual destination was.

In the beginning, when my father noticed it, they laughed it off and thought that it was cute, but this went on for about 6 months and it was constant and persistent. It started to get out of hand when I apparently began insisting that my father took the same route when he carried me. That's when they realized that something was not right. The next time I was on one of my excursions along the hub and spoke, my father started telling me to take a different route, to which I was apparently unyielding, so they made it a point to show me, and teach me and they kept doing this for another two months.

Then they started to notice that it got worse. Whereas before I had to walk along established paths, and would sometimes take the effort to establish a path, now I had stopped making new paths and wouldn't go to any part of the house that did not already have a path. That's when my father put his foot down. What came next was painful for everyone.

He moved the furniture around, blocked off my central hub, and made me go to different points in the house. That was supported by a firm and loud voice (which I was not used to) and slowly they broke me of it. When I started to get back to the obsession of routes, they would move the furniture again and they would make me go to parts of the house that I didn't want to go to.

That did it. It broke my dependence on obsessions. What my father instinctively knew, according to my mother, was that those paths had become my safety zones and I was just doing what I felt safe with. He taught me (more than most kids would have needed, I am sure) is that I had to face my fears. Those of us with ASD have safe zones because we have a heightened sense of survival.

Just so you know how that turned out for me – ever since that time, I guess, I have noted many fears that have triggered in me and the lesson my father administered always came to the rescue. I faced everything that I feared. For instance, the first time I was supposed to board a plane, I was so racked with fear that I left, and didn't get on. I took the train instead. To counter it, I went to the closest airfield and found a flight school and got a flight instructor to take me up in a small plane. I paid him for the whole day because I knew it would take a while. It took me 90 minutes just to get the courage to get in the plane and shut the door, and another 30 minutes on the apron with the engine running. Mac was a really patient old timer and he just let me get my stomach together and took off only when I was ready. I was in such fear and I just kept fighting the sensation one heartbeat at a time. To cut a long story short, I pushed myself to look out the window and stare the height down and to fight the fear while I told my brain that it was ok. We landed one hour and forty minutes later.

I no longer have the fear to fly. I managed to rewire my brain.

The brain is a wonderful thing, I have learnt. You don't have to carry through life what you are endowed with at birth. It is malleable. You can mold your brain – the physical one to adapt and to conform, if you like, or to stand out, if you wish. It's called neuroplasticity, and that is the phenomenon that my father relied on when he saw that I was doing something that would be a problem down the road – and he stepped in to change it.

I wanted to relate this story because most of the symptoms I have had since youth that point to the external presumption of ASD, I have molded into something else. I've learnt how to counter my fear. I've even learnt how to cope with my inability, fear and repulsion to socialize in a room full of people. I have successfully brought two works together in my mind. I tell you this because I am about to lay out for you the various traits that typify ASD, and when you see them, some may ring a bell, others may not initially, but then you may recognize its shadow. The thing that I want you to remember is that you can change that to the degree you wish so, if you are reading this book to understand yourself or to understand a loved one, remember this is not a sentence passed down on you for life, it is merely a work in progress and you just have to put the finishing touches to it.

Common Traits of ASD

Here are the generic lists of traits that manifest in various shades among those with ASD:

1. Challenges in reading the emotion or expressions of people, including body language and facial cues.
2. Challenges in presenting appropriate emotions.
3. Unable to start or extend two-way conversations, but could go on talking without realizing the lack of interest in the other person.
4. Safety in routines and rituals to the point of obsession.
5. Finds comfort in a limited range of activities.

6. Preference for compulsive behavior – like strict schedules or rituals.

Keep in mind though that just because you have one of these, it doesn't put you on the spectrum. If you have already been diagnosed, it's because you have a combination of these factors to varying degrees and various paths to manifestation, but every single one of these can be mitigated if you put your mind to it and teach yourself to handle it differently.

Genetic Issues

It has also been determined that there are distinct genetic differences between those who have been diagnosed with ASD, and those who have not, but the research in this area is still fairly nascent, and more needs to be understood before we can start to screen for this condition genetically.

Chapter 2: Maybe I am Autistic, Now What?

Well, you have looked at that list and you have taken a test online to see if you fall within the definition. Just do a search online and you will get a list of sites that you can go to. You will see that most of them have similar questions. Get one that actually scores the answers. There are some out there that give you the questions, and then tell you what the answers should be and how to score it. That's just too much of a waste of time. Find one that scores it and look at your score. If you are past 30, well there is a good chance that you are somewhere on the spectrum.

If you got to this stage, you are at the fork in the road. On one side, you have to think about getting further tests done, and, on the other side, you do nothing. Yes, that is indeed the option. You can choose to do nothing, especially if you are already an adult, and you have grown into your ways. I remember when I was first diagnosed; it was a bit of a distraction because there was now this label hanging over my head. I didn't feel any different than the day before I was diagnosed, yet there was this sudden drag on my mind. If I had to do it all over again, I wouldn't move forward with a test. I will explain the testing diagnosis process in Chapter 4 for those of you that are thinking about going through with it.

On the other hand, if your current life is difficult, by this, what I mean, is that you suspect that ASD is involved, you've taken the online assessments and they are in the high numbers and you are not sure how to proceed, then taking the test would be a good option for you because it opens you up to the certainty that will propel you to seek guidance.

The decision to move forward with a full diagnosis depends, in my opinion, on three factors.

1. To what degree are you limited in your daily activities?
2. Your state of peace and happiness.
3. If you need help in coping.

If you are not at all affected by it, or by the time you find out, you have already acclimatized, and then you really don't need to deal with the label. Getting a label put on your situation - something that you have already learned to deal with all your life - is only going to get complicated. The self-fulfilling prophecy that the label creates will actually expand your symptoms, and bring to the surface things that have actually been kept dormant.

On the other hand, if you have one or more of the situations already manifesting in your day-to-day life, then getting a full diagnosis would be the prudent course of action. With a full diagnosis, you will be able to get expert advice on how to handle the symptoms.

There is no cure for this, and you need to understand that this is a quality of life issue. If your quality of life can be improved by going further, then go for it; otherwise, keep doing what you've been doing all this time.

You must understand that those diagnosed with ADS are not consequentially less intelligent. You may have difficulty speaking or keeping your sentence straight, but your mind would be fully functional. Until today, I have had a few occasions where my sentences get jumbled up, or my conversation is not fully as intended. I find that taking a deep breath, slowing things down and then getting back to it helps.

Remember that all of what you face under the influence of ADS comes from your brain. As I've said, because your brain is moldable, you can train it to perceive and react differently. One of the things that I always found in myself was that my first exposure to things was never perfect, but, with a little focus and effort, I would be able to do better. We have a very high sense of survival and we tend to be cautious of everything. That causes a secondary response to most stimuli while the manifestation of fear in various inward and outwardly states. Don't confuse those secondary conditions with ASD.

If you are in the middle and you think you should move further but your gut is telling you otherwise, I suggest one additional step before you go for a full assessment. First off, don't let the possibility, or even the diagnosis of ASD bring you down. It's not the end of the world, and it certainly is not something that you just contracted. If you are diagnosed with it as an adult, it just means you have had it for a while and you are attaching a name to it now. Instead, remember you are attaching what you have grown up with to the name. You are not attaching your brain to the generic definition that is an aggregate of what all of us already have. It is unique to you, so there is nothing to freak out about.

So, here you stand, fresh with the experience of just finding out, or just coming to suspect that, after all this time, you are maybe autistic. What happens next? Well, in my experience, the answer lies within you and, by that, I do not intend to make this sound cryptic.

By this, I literally mean that the answers of what to do next must come from within you, and they must be based on what your objectives are, and what your core strengths have been all this time.

In my case, before I knew of my diagnosis, I always made the effort to mold my brain to my will. If I was afraid of flying, I got on a plane and didn't come down until I got over it or rationalized it. When I was afraid of a roomful of people, I joined a toastmaster's club. I made sure that I wrestled my nature-given brain into learning how to be at peace.

After all, what all of you can agree with is that the thorn in our side that prevents us from doing anything, or the whip on our backs that prods us to do something, has always been about the feeling of peace. When I was in fear, that peace was destabilized. When I got over that fear, the peace returned.

That brings me to my next chapter on how to rethink things and how to will your brain into shape.

Chapter 3: Rethinking and Realizing

Whether you are ASD or not, you have to always strive to be better than whom you are. Not doing that will render you forever as a child. I was in Cleveland the other day, and was having breakfast at Denny's when this older guy came in, walking slowly, and sat at the counter. My waitress greeted him while standing at my table, and he waved back. She turned back and apologized to me and explained that this old man was nearly 80, had a stroke about five years back and lost the use of his entire right side but he wouldn't accept it, and he insisted on therapy and he taught himself how to walk and be independent. He succeeded. After approximately 2 years, he could walk and do the things he wanted to, albeit a little slow – but that was more a function of his age than due to the stroke.

What he had successfully done is to bypass all the brain cells that died in the stroke – which happened to control his motor skills on the right side, and he taught himself how to do everything from scratch.

What does this have to do with ASD?

ASD is a developmental disability. Things happen to us in ways that are different from how it happens to others. Some areas are slower, some areas are more pronounced, but, regardless of what our brains look like, it is up to us to teach it to be the way we want it to be.

Maybe this sudden realization that you have ASD is the thing you needed to get you on track, and to do the things that you once didn't think were possible because of whatever reason. Now you have a reason to pin it to, and you know it's a brain development effect, so what you have to do is learn different ways to develop your brain.

Each person learns skills differently. Some learn by theory, others learn by doing it hands-on. There are so many variations, but, because of mass education, the way we are taught in school is standardized. That doesn't make it right or wrong, it just makes it the most effective method to teach the most amount of kids. Those who have abilities outside that perimeter aren't able to keep up and so they develop differently – unfortunately that is referred to as developing slowly.

I remember I used to have so much trouble keeping up in school. I would do really well in maths, but in English and history, I would stumble. Like I said, my parents didn't know (we all didn't) about anything called ASD, they just found ways to solve the problem. When I wasn't getting English, my father sat me down and started using flash cards. At first it didn't do much, but then suddenly I realized that I was able to remember and I was able to repeat words. I then found out that the faster he got, the more I remembered, up to a point. Anything beyond that and I would lose track, so there was an optimal speed.

He tried that with history and it worked there as well. I was slower in school – but he didn't label it as slow, he just figured I learnt differently and he was right. It took a lot of effort on his part, and on mine, but it was worth every second of it. My father didn't believe in labeling the problem, he believed in solving it and he would go about trying whatever he could until the problem was solved.

It turns out ASD, for me, was not about being slower, it was about being faster. All we needed to do was keep me from getting bored. My father found how to keep me engaged and then I started to learn.

I also found a coping mechanism. One of the things with my brand of ASD back then was that I was hypersensitive to data streams. I absorbed everything and, because I didn't know how to handle all that information, I started blocking them out. That's probably why some kids seem despondent. It's not that they don't get it; it's that they are tuning things out because no-one has taught them to manage the incoming data streams. I was taught to manage it, not shut it out, and that worked to my advantage. By knowing how to handle incoming streams of data, I was able to observe more and that is always a good thing. Talking is over-rated and you shouldn't worry too much if you are not the communicative type. Unless you plan on becoming a politician, talking is not necessarily something you should miss.

I found that my silence in conversations became a powerful tool. It allowed me to observe and remember the details better than sitting down and transcribing notes. It was another example of how to do mental *judo* on my predicament – take an opponent and use their force to flip them over. Every time I am faced with a limitation, I just rethink my position, shift my stance and I use what I have. It has worked brilliantly for me so far.

Chapter 4: The Process of Diagnosis

We've already touched on the ASD assessment, so we will skip over that while illuminating on the process of diagnosis. Once there is an indication that you may have autism, and you have pondered on the next step, you would have come to one of two conclusions: to proceed with the full diagnosis, or to leave it as is because you don't see how it can alter or improve your quality of life.

In the event you chose the former, it is then time to further the evaluation with specific professionals. The first thing you need to do is visit with a doctor to get a referral to one of three specialists.

The doctor will be able to give you the best alternative of whether it should be a psychiatrist, psychologist, or a neurologist, but, mind you, if you start by visiting the psychologist, he may further refer you to a neurologist.

In my case they referred me to a psychologist and after an interview, a detailed questionnaire and some tests; the psychologist confirmed what the initial assessment had revealed.

There are two possible routes that your assessment can take. The first is that your primary caregiver refers you to one of the three specialists. They make an assessment and they come to the conclusion that you are within the autism spectrum, and that's that.

The second possible path this could take is that after the initial assessment, your GP sends you to one of the three specialists and, after that evaluation, they, in turn, send you to one more specialist for additional work-up, including a possible MRI. The neurologist will further make a diagnosis of the physical aspects of the disorder in your case.

Now, there are two things you need to take away from this. The first is that there is a physical difference in your brain when it comes to ASD. With a sufficiently precise scan, there are some methods that can detect some variances and they will be able to detect exactly the extent of the variation in the brain. In some cases, that may not be visible or detectable, but the effect that the altered brain has on behavior is studied by the psychologist or the psychiatrist.

The second thing you need to take away from this is that even though there is a genetic link to this, it is not fully known and fully understood, and so it's more like looking at a shadow to determine the shape of the original object. The MRI will be able to give a better understanding of the condition.

Then comes the final step in the process which is to determine the level of your ASD. Like I said, in my case, I was deemed to be on the autistic spectrum, but there are two other classifications that could be made, and each has similar roots. While these roots are similar, their subtle difference can make all the difference.

The final diagnosis could be that you have one of three conditions: ASD, an autistic disorder, or Asperger's syndrome. It is important to keep in mind that they are not separate conditions, just the same general condition with specific differences. There is a good reason why the three are separated in the diagnosis – it helps medical professionals and the people who help them better manage the effects and symptoms.

Regardless of the category that you fall under, there is one advantage that you possess in finding out now. That advantage is that you have lived your life all this time as a neurotypical person. Just because those same characteristics are now called autistic does not mean that you are disadvantaged in any way. If anything, those classifications help you to understand better the areas of shortfall in your life that you have noticed in the past, but now can explain clearly. For the longest time I used to jumble my typewritten words. There were always specific patterns to them, and I never could fathom the reason behind that quirk – now I do. That has allowed me to look at it as something I need to (and can) fix; and because I know neuroplasticity allows me to do this, I have taken the necessary steps to correct.

It is normal for some of you to feel depressed and out of sorts upon learning of your diagnosis but really, what's changed? Nothing. You are the same person you were yesterday, but that is more easily said than done.

In some cases, finding out may trigger secondary issues. Depression is common among some who feel like their whole world has changed because of this new label. The psychiatric side effects of finding out have the likelihood of extending the autism effects. Learning and socializing depends a lot on the lack of fear and that is one of the main reasons we keep away because of our fear in various areas. The confirmation that we are different in terms of the diagnosis compounds that fear and robs us of the self-confidence that we may have built up over the years. Finding out you have ASD is nothing like finding out one has cancer. One will change your life, the other won't.

The biggest fear I had was sharing the information and the diagnosis with my friends and family. I was convinced no-one needed to know, but, at the same time, it felt like I had to tell them. This question took me some time and I expect it will take you some time as well. My thoughts on it are in the next chapter.

Once all that is done, the next phase of it is looking inside and accepting yourself for who you are. If you feel beat up about the fact you are not autistic, don't feel bad about wanting to feel that way. It's normal. As human beings, one of the ways our brain works is by attaching meanings to words. It's the same way that if you keep telling a kid he is smart, the brain slowly starts to conform and he does what he has to do to get smart. If you tell a person that they are worthless, in time, they will start believing that is true and they will behave in a way that reflects that analysis.

When you tell a person he or she is autistic, then you find that they start to take on traits that are stereotypical of the disorder. That is the one thing that you cannot do, and that is the downside of finding out. There is a lot of upside to knowing, so, instead of avoiding the diagnosis, accept it and embrace it. It takes some time but the truth will, indeed, set you free. We will look at that in further detail in Chapter 6.

Finally, once you are diagnosed, it is an interesting thing to look at all the different things that characterized the disorder. I started on a process of discovery and found that many of the things that were distinctive about me were caused by ASD. I found that my nature of never dating and only doing so was when the girl was bold enough to ask me out. Autism manifests in many different ways. People ascribe the state of being shy to autistic people, but we are not shy, it just manifests in that way perhaps but, that is not the only way it manifests. For me, I was not shy to ask a woman out, I just felt that it was beneath me to do all the things that men do to get a woman's attention, so I didn't, but then I met my wife and all that went out the door, and I asked her to go out with me and even asked her to marry me. When it became absolutely necessary, I broke the shackles of ASD and did what I had to. We will look at relationships and sexual issues in Chapter 6 as well, and you will be surprised to find that being autistic has some significant advantages.

Associated Psychiatric Issues

There are four associated psychiatric issues you need to think about and evaluate if there has been any trace of it in your life, and how you can proceed to overcome it. Some may have one, two, or even a combination of all four psychiatric issues and what is needed is an understanding of how the cocktail manifests in you.

The four associated issues are: ADHD (Attention Deficit and Hyperactivity Disorder), bipolar disorder, schizophrenia, and depression. None of these conditions will allow you to have the peace that you deserve. There are two ways that you can counter these issues.

The first is to seek professional medical attention. That really is your first thought and you have to evaluate a number of issues when it comes to that. I didn't need professional help because I felt I was already at peace with myself and happy with my strengths, habits and achievements.

The second thing you have to do, and this is the thing that I have relied on for most of my life, is the power of meditation and mindfulness. I haven't come into a situation or a state of being that is not easily and totally controlled by invoking the state of mindfulness and meditation.

Meditation and Mindfulness

I am not going to get into meditation and mindfulness in any deep and extended way because it may distract the reader from the point of this book, but I will say that the topic is something that you should look into and advance. I have been practicing it since before I even knew about autism, or even came close to thinking that I may be autistic.

Meditation has helped me to balance what I need to focus on, and to adjust the frequency of my mind to the level that I need. My tendencies to obsess on a certain thing, or my fears, when irrational, have mostly been managed and curtailed by the power of meditation.

One of the things that I found hard to cope with is the way that language dictates how we behave. I mentioned that earlier in the book. The words you use, the words that others use on you, and the words you use to describe yourself are all tools that alter the way you think and behave. The word autism seems to have a negative effect and that is probably because of the way society, in general, frames the issue. We are not here to debate the politics of autism; however, there is an effect in the way it is perceived and the stigma it bestows, and I find that meditation helps me to scrub away the effects of that stigma and the stereotype.

On the other hand, mindfulness is the real star of the show. Mindfulness was the key trait that I learned from my parents that allowed me to avoid the tendency to overdo things or be compulsive in my actions. Mindfulness was the fix I needed to overcome compulsive habits. Compulsion was one of my issues. I tended to do things over and over again for two reasons. One I would 'forget' that I had done them and the other was that I worried that I didn't do them well enough. When I started to learn mindfulness, my conscious memory of acts that I performed started to improve, and that automatically prevented me from doing things again. It also allowed me to pay attention to what I was doing and do that act well, so that I started to get confidence that the job was well done, and my peace about these acts improved.

Meditation and mindfulness are ways to keep your mind strong, and to keep yourself from falling into the depression trap.

Chapter 5: Sharing Your Diagnosis With Friends and Family

You could say that the hardest thing I had to do was tell my family. The truth is that it was hard because of what I thought of what they would think. When I actually got down to telling them, the only thing I proved was that I underestimated my family. I did lose a couple of friends though and I never really understood why. Be prepared for that and don't let it bother you. There is always attrition in all things we do. I remember losing some family members when I got married, so it's not a big deal – people come and go in your life. What matters is that you stay in your lane, and they stay in theirs.

As far as my family was concerned (wife and kids), they took it really well. My son laughed and said that he always knew that there was something wrong with me, but that was purely in jest. In all seriousness, he told me that I am the same person that I was before the diagnosis, and you have to keep telling yourself that every day.

As for my wife, she found a new form of prodding me and making fun of my quirks. It turned into a joke and I was fine with that because, in all seriousness, if you can't laugh at it, then what else are you going to do? The rest of the world treats it serious enough and beyond the limits of it being such a devastating matter. It's not. I understand that I shouldn't be making sweeping statements because there are various grades of functionality in those of us with ASD. I still have high functionality and some people have less, but here is what you have to understand – you are who you are, and when you realize you need to stop conforming or stop succumbing to other's definition, you will be all the better for it.

You also have to be vigilant on how you receive, perceive and internalize what anyone says to you about you – regardless of whether it is about autism, or about the way you chew your food. There is critique and then there is pity and criticism. I respond better to the former and abhor the latter.

Sharing your diagnosis with those around you is your choice. My concern when I chose to share it was about how they may feel. As the father and husband, I have always wanted to keep my family safe and secure and my fear was that by telling them they would lose that sense of peace that comes from being safe and feeling secure.

Here are five things you need to consider when deciding to share your diagnosis with family and friends:

1. Are they emotionally strong enough to see it for what it is and not freak out over what it is not?
2. Do they rely on you for emotional and structural support exclusively?
3. Are they fairly well informed, or do they have irrational beliefs and superstitions?
4. Are your children too young to comprehend the matter?
5. Are they going to worry about you?

These are five obvious issues and they stretch across the board to all adults who are diagnosed. You need to balance this against the notion that they have the right to know. In my personal opinion, if my condition was so serious that it was degenerative, I would condition them and then let them know, but autism is not degenerative.

To condition them, you need to understand three specific areas of your new life (new, because you have this new definition hanging over you) and that is you have to understand yourself. Second, you need to understand the scope and extent of ASD. By this, I mean you need to go out and read as much as you can about the clinical issues, the psychological issues, the emotional issues, and the experiences of those who are out there. When all that is said and done, you are ready to look at the third issue.

The third issue is about the intersection between what you know (or think you know) about yourself and what you now know about autism. They are never one and the same, but you can look at the intersection when they meet and you will now have three tasks to accomplish.

1. The first is to understand what part of your personality is the real you – the part that you have hoped, dreamed, wished and experienced. You will need to do some serious soul-searching and this is where the meditation comes in handy.
2. The second task is to look at your limitations and divide them into three:
   a. The areas that you have not tried to accomplish.

    b. The areas you have tried but failed for some reason.
    c. The areas that you have overcome and eventually succeeded with.
3. The third and final task is to look at the areas that bring you peace and the areas that disturb your peace. By understanding your peace profile, you will be able to understand what motivates you and what holds you back.

Once you understand this framework, it is easy to understand the areas that are dominated by your autism. This will dovetail nicely with the research that you have conducted in the time before coming to this part of the process. Remember, knowledge is key. The more you know, the better you get at overcoming your limitations and, the more you overcome your limitations, the more confidence you have. The more confidence you have, the more you will be able to dive your potential and, one day, you will stop and look back and all you see are a string of successes and none of it looks like what the stigma of autism said it would.

Sharing your diagnosis with friends and family from a position of strength is not a bad thing. It is very different from the situation where parents find out that their toddler is autistic but, as an adult, the game is different. When you imbue strength, it comes across and bolsters those who rely on you.

Sharing your diagnosis also has positive effects. One of the things that you should do is make the ground rules - that there should be no pity. Trade pity for understanding. Pity is a corrosive response and not one you should expect from your loved ones. If there is any that crops up, you should nip it in the bud. The positive effect that you can expect, however, is that you now have the opportunity to accept input and instruction.

The first thing that my wife did when she found out about my diagnosis was exhaustively research the issue. She quickly and meticulously went through a process of elimination of all the things that she knew I exhibited, and what she was left with were some areas that seemed to be a part of me which has a part of the autism. She then went through that list and dropped all the areas that had a positive impact in my life – and there were quite a few. What was left was a short list of things that we now knew were rooted in autism and were holding me back in areas that we had not thought about.

We then attacked it together, one by one. It was the most amazing thing anyone has ever done for me, but it was also the most amazing experience as I found new strength in areas I didn't know was possible. This anecdote is not about how to handle your issues (you can take it that way if you like), but it is more to tell you that if you share your diagnosis with someone who is able to share their strength in their effort to help straighten you out, it would do the two of you a lot of good. She told me once, sometime after we did this exercise, that she is glad this happened because it gave us something to grow and work on. And I agree.

My two kids, on the other hand, started researching this and started to consider what the genetic issues would be for them. After the research and some soul searching, they announced to my wife and me that they feel fairly confident that they didn't get the gene and that we should not worry that they may be affected. It was an amazing experience to see my family come together, and that made me really glad that I had chosen to tell them.

Sharing your diagnosis is not just about you, it's about alerting your family so that they have the necessary information to make the necessary judgments about things. One thing that you must not do is make the announcement and leave everyone to their own devices. They need to see the strength in you and let that strength mirror back so that you can get strength from them because, while it may not be the autism that affects your daily life, it could be the depression that creeps in and then it starts to shatter the peace.

Chapter 6: Self-Acceptance and Discovery

We touched this and a few other areas that you should consider looking at in your endeavor to dive deeper into autism. What you want to do is dive deeper into understanding yourself and then finding a reason for the things you do.

There is a phrase that always rings in my head – *"The truth will set you free."* It's one of those phrases that pops in and out of my head on a constant basis. I find that it means a lot of different things to different people. They interpret that as a way to not tell lies. They can interpret that as an instruction to find freedom in telling the truth, and, in some cases, people take it too far and can tell you straight to your face that you look ugly – under the auspices of telling the truth.

In my experience, I have come to take it to mean (and this is just for me) that the truth is in knowing things as they are without the bells and whistles that make you feel good about something or by sugar coating something just to make it palatable.

It has been a habit of mine to get to the nut of things and to see it for what it is. I have no patience for people who hem and haw about things that take time in getting to the truth, so I like to be served the truth so that I can save time in analyzing it and I can respond appropriately to the event.

Autism is the same to me. I want it straight to my face and, whatever the issue, I want to handle it with both eyes wide open. It is said that President Lincoln would fill his cabinet with critics as much as he would his allies. The reason for it was that he believed, and rightfully so, that you can always rely on your critics to tell it like it is, especially when you get it wrong. That's what you want – that's the truth – and indeed, it will set you free, but you have to have the guts to take it.

For those with autism, having the guts is not always something that we are known for because we are, by nature, cautious. In time, as we mature, that caution in all things starts to pay off, and that reward makes caution a habit. When caution is habitual, it becomes the spark of fear and fear then grows into anxiety and anxiety shakes us off our peace.

The only way to overcome that is to separate caution from fear and to fortify our understanding of all things with knowledge. You need to know and you need to seek out the truth in all things.

The second layer of truth is to know the physical limits of yourself. Let me put it this way. The interesting thing about light is that it is part of the electromagnetic spectrum and it ranges from gamma rays to radio waves. We only get to detect visible light which is a small percentage of the spectrum. The rest is just one big blind spot. Are we handicapped? Just because we are unable to see it or detect it didn't stop us, so what did we do? We invented ways of detecting it.

In the same way, autism leaves us with a few blind spots. What we have to do is find ways to get around that, but it takes a tremendous amount of effort. I found that some things took me a tremendous effort, and some things I was used to. If I really reflect, I can recall even the things that come easily to me now, had a little effort put into them in the beginning because of my ASD. Like the thing about fear of flying – which was a combination of fear of heights, and the incomplete knowledge of flight; once I learned how it worked and sat in the plane that went up, I was no longer afraid. That was a significant amount of effort to get to that point. As such, the point to take away from this is that it takes more effort for us to do something that is in our blind spot, and that holds true for everyone, as the difference is that we (those diagnosed with ASD) have a large blind spot. Our process of overcoming that is why we have to constantly be on the path of discovery. We are constantly applying effort to discover things about ourselves and the way we fit in the world. That, by no means, suggests that we are looking to conform, it just means that we are trying to make the most of our assets.

As we keep going through this process, we start to realize that we are comfortable in our skin. That's an important aspect in all of this. We need to first accept who and what we are, and that, by no means, includes a definition of being autistic. Just because we don't see the infrared light in the electromagnetic spectrum, doesn't mean we need to call ourselves blind. This is not about being in denial; it's about focusing on our strengths and advancing that.

Sexual Issues

One of the things that you need to have a 'heads up' about is the sexual nature of those with ASD. This is not about your sexual preference or appetite. That seems to span across the ASD population with the same pattern as it does in the neurotypical population.

But the point that is a little different, is the prerequisites that occur in a person who is autistic. As much as it seems that we are distant from people and non-engaging in any way, we are actually not that way with those we love, even if we do not necessarily show it openly.

We tend to require a sense of emotional and cerebral closeness before the path to intimacy can be tread upon. If this is you, or it is you inside, then remember that there is nothing wrong with that. It may a be a bit hard in high school and college when the normal kids create an atmosphere of pressure, but, as an adult, that kind of emotional intimacy mixes well with physical intimacy.

One of the things that affects our peace is the need to conform to the way others tend to do things and this is one of those areas. You don't have to do the same things, you just need to be true to your own self and take part in things under your own terms.

Here are some of the things that will resonate with those diagnosed with ASD:

- A deep sense of self-respect and self-confidence with your partner.
- The build-up of respect for your partner (or potential partner).
- A connection that is deeper than casual relationships with your partner.
- The ability to have frank and open communication with your partner.
- A significant level of trust with your partner.

For those who are not married, it may give you peace to know that many people diagnosed with ASD remain single or remain celibate by choice in their life. It is not because they are not accepted by a willing partner or they are not capable of sexual performance. The reason is that they are unable to find anyone who will give them the deep-needed bond of a relationship as a prerequisite of sex.

Relationships with autistic people are wholesome in the sense that we tend to see the person not the act, and tend to value respect not the experience. Of course that's nature; nurture on the other hand could alter that, but the instinct inside to be that way doesn't change. There are forces outside that could push us off from whom we really are and that's true for other areas of an autistic's life.

Sex, intimacy and relationships are all intertwined in our life. Everything an autistic person does, comes with thought and consideration and it is not usually taken lightly. Our nature to be cautious forces us to evaluate all things – sometimes to the point of excess.

To be able to make your diagnosis of autism work in your favor, learn up about it, do whatever it takes to build your confidence and quit trying to conform on things that do not need conformity. We are the quintessential individual; we stand out in a crowd and have no natural instinct to want to be a part of it. What we really want is to have normalcy and that sometimes confuses us.

Every day I wake up, I start to realize that I am grateful for the strengths I possess and that would not be possible if it wasn't for autism. I was lucky to find my niche in life because my parents were relentless in their effort to maintain my individuality, yet overcome my fears and habits.

Concluding Thoughts

I hope you have found a sliver of what you were looking for, and even if you weren't looking for anything specific, I hope you managed to take away a few things from this short path through my personal jungle.

If all else takes time to apply, know this: the only thing that you need to strive for is the acquisition and maintenance of peace. Whatever effort you put into it, with the goal to attain and maintain that peace, you will not be disappointed. You will find the strength you need to put in the physical effort to do certain things that others around you seem to do without the slightest thought – but therein lies your strength. You need to apply your mind in creative ways to be able to overcome the particular shortfall that is endemic of an autistic soul.

I urge you to read what's out there, but take care in how far you let mere definitions and descriptions mold your mind and your personality. The answers you need are in the same place I found my answers – mostly on the inside and in the words of loved ones who didn't think I was any different from the fact that I was diagnosed with something that is described in ways that is nothing like me.

I remember reading about autism and ASD and all the other psychological challenges that are out there, and not once did I think that I was autistic because the description presented in most places was nothing that resonated with me.

Only when I took the test did I find out that I have this thing so, in actuality, it didn't change my life when I didn't know it, and it didn't get me too down when I found out. It did help me see things in a different light, and that had a positive impact on my life.

I read a lot about how depression is the thing that follows soon after adults find out that they have ASD. I can see that. Our minds are funny in certain ways, but it doesn't have to be. Nothing has really changed and, unless you let a word define who you are, this word should not have an impact.

The best way to deal with it is to reflect. I call it meditation in this book, but you can call it whatever you want. It is just the process of letting the natural powers of your mind sort through things. You just have to keep your anxiety and emotions out of it.

Remember that however tough it is for you, and I know it varies for each of us, you have to remember one simple fact that our brains are malleable. Use the proven fact that neuroplasticity works in our favor, and put in the effort and consistency to bring about the change that you need to bring peace into your life. I only urge you to use the power of change to make the change for something lasting, and not for something fleeting. You have the gift of seeing things differently, so use it.

After you read this book and you feel that you are not keen on telling others that you have autism, that's your choice. Usually, your instinct is something that you should learn to listen to. No-one, even others in your same situation, can't tell you what is best. I am just sharing what has transpired in my life and how it relates to me. If it works for you, great.

The one thing that never worked for me, was doing nothing. When I did nothing, I regressed. When I did something, I inevitably moved forward and I like moving forward. I like finding out what I can do and what more I can experience.

I've come to a point that I bungee jump even though it scares the life out of me when I am at the ledge. I do it because it reminds me that I am in charge, not my fears, not my cautionary state and not my play-it-safe self. Me, I am in charge of who, what, when and how. That is empowering for me and it gives me the energy to put in the effort that I need to overcome potential limitations.

What I find is that we all start somewhere; that includes Einstein, Newton, Hawking and a whole host of people that I've not even heard of. We all start somewhere, and, as we bounce around this universe looking for our place in it, we can hardly do anything, but the moment we stumble upon peace, our world and our place in it materialize and we start to make a difference.

Aside from wanting to experience peace, what we want in this world is to make a difference. However small, that is the wish we all have – to touch this world in the short period that we are here, and to leave it a little better off when we leave. Our greatest sadness when we find out about our autism is that we think we can't make that difference and we are no longer able to contribute to anything. That is not true, not even in the least. We have so much to contribute if we are willing to put in the effort and put in the special perspective we have.

With that, I shall leave you to chart your own path to peace with the hope that some of what I say may pave the way, even if just for a few steps.

Peace!

Glossary

Asperger's Syndrome: It is a collection of clinical signs involving abnormal social, language and play skills mostly affecting children with a high-functioning form of autism.

Auditory Processing Disorder: It is a clinical condition that affects the ability of affected patients to process speech from other people. Affected children face difficulty of distinguishing subtle differences between sounds in words.

Autism: It is a condition that captures a wide spectrum of disorders referred to as pervasive developmental disorders or autism spectrum disorders. ASD or PDD are a collection of neurological developmental disorders that interfere with a child's ability to express themselves, socialize with others, imagine and learn.

Awareness: This the ability of one to comprehend, perceive, feel or recognize their situation, surrounding or environment.

Caregiver: Is a person (mother, relative, father or any family member) who takes responsibility or full care of someone (Sick, elderly or paralyzed) or a child who cannot carefully for themselves. They provide ensure healthy and appropriate well-being of affected autistic children who cannot take care of themselves.

Clinical practice: This is a framework of practice that consist of those actions, procedures or activities that clinicians carry with and on behalf of patients, especially those activities undertaken in the patient's presence and with patient's cooperation.

Communications: The application or expression of non-verbal cues and verbal actions to convey ideas to facilitate interaction and exchange of information. The mostly applied non-verbal cues include eye-gaze, facial expression and verbal behaviors used are speech.

Compulsions: compulsions mostly encompass activities such as cleaning, counting and checking done through intentional repetitive behaviors that follow specific rules.

Developmental Milestones: These are beacons of development that allow clinicians to map out and assess expected and appropriate child's development, learning and behavior. They entail behaviors or skills that most children are expected to display at a particular age.

Diagnosis: Diagnosis is the problem or condition that affects the patient that clinicians arrive at after observing and eliciting clinical signs and symptoms, laboratory investigations and imaging studies. Diagnosis of ASD is done through observation of behavioral features using the DSM-IV-TR model. A team of professionals use the guideline to elicit information about the child's growth and medical history, behaviors and activity.

Early Indicators of Autism: These are early or initial signs that indicate a child might have autism such as children failure to respond to their names, lack of eye contact, absent joint attention and involvement in repetitive movement patterns.

Early Intervention: These are measures clinicians take at the initial stages or start of a disease process to control or prevent further damage or impairment of person functionality.

Echolalia: This is a clinical sign when a patient repeat phrases, words, sounds or intonation of the speech of other people. Echolalia is a common presentation in children with ASD when they try to learn how to talk. Echolalia can either be immediate (immediately after the speech is heard) or delayed (later after hearing the speech)

Epidemiology: The scientific study of distribution and determinants of health-related states and events in a particular population. Epidemiology captures the incidence and prevalence of a disease conditions in a given population at specific time.

Expressive Language: The application of speech or verbal cues to convey thoughts, ideas and feelings to other people. People use words and sounds to communicate their message to others.

Eye Gaze: it involves observing other peoples face to identify and see what they are viewing and indicate interest in engaging. It is a non-verbal behavior applied to convey a message devoid of use of words.

Functional Play: Refers to the application of objects by children for their designed or normal use. Example includes for instance rolling a ball.

Genetics: It is a scientific branch concerned with the study of heredity, genetic variations and genes in living organisms. Genetics helps in identifying or mapping out some health conditions that can be passed on from parents to their offspring.

Gesture: They entail specific and understood movement patterns involving the hands and head to alert, signal or convey information to someone. Some examples include greeting through hand waving or refusal or agreeing through head shaking. They are non-verbal behaviors intended to pass information or express feelings without use of speech.

Healthy Development: The expected growth and acquisition of skills progression of a child with regards to physical, mental and social development of a child within specified time limits.

Hype responsiveness: This is an exaggerated sensitivity or abnormal reactivity to sensory input. The patient feels and reacts in unusual way to stimuli most people would react to in a normal way.

Interactions: This involves socializing and engaging with people and the environment through learning, communication, imagination and emotions.

Joint Attention: Refers to behavior pattern of children during their first year of life to spontaneously share attention with others normally first recognized by their caregivers. This ability is recognized when infants shift their gaze between object of their interest, the caregiver and back to the object, following the gaze of the caregiver and applying gestures to draw attention others attention to the object in question.

Mental Disorders: These are disorders which involve behavioral or mental patterns that result in significant distress or impairment of personal functioning through disrupting their various mental faculties. Common mental disorders include schizophrenia, dementia, Alzheimer and Parkinson's disease.

Misconceptions: These are abstractive ideas, concerns, statements, conclusions or beliefs that are false or misguided since they rely on faulty reason, thinking or comprehension.

Newly Diagnosed: it is basically a recent or new diagnosis of a particular condition based on clinical, laboratory or imaging investigations. Autism can be a new diagnosis if previously normal child start to display features of autism.

Nonfunctional Routines: These are repeated activities or behaviors that autistic children participate in that are particular, sequential and purposeless. Examples entails always arranging play toys in an orderly fashion each time instead of playing with them.

Non-Verbal Signs: They encompass a spectrum of behavior patterns such as facial expression, gestures or eye gaze. People who understand and can interpret their meaning apply these behavior patterns to convey or exchange information or express emotions without the use of speech

Over Reactivity to Sensory input: It is an exaggerated sensitivity or hyper responsiveness to sensory stimuli. The patient presents with unusual response to a normal or ordinary stimulus for most people.

Phrases: Phrase is a short group of words with some special or particular meaning or other significance when used together. Example of a phrase, it is raining cats and dogs.

Pointing: The behavior gesture pattern of the index figure to implore for an object or to attract attention to an object or comment on it or share interest in it. Example is a child pointing to swinging balloon with intentions to share interest in it.

Pretend Play: The ability of children during their developmental stages to use their imaginations in performing certain tasks and to be something or someone else. A child can imagine being a driver driving a toy car.

Regulation of Emotions: Refers to children ability to process and adjust their emotions or behavior in response to external stimuli and internal stimuli. Example of external stimuli includes temperature while internal stimuli involve thoughts among others.

Repetitive Mannerisms: These refer

to behavioral repetitive movement patterns or body positions such as hand flapping or body rocking. Autistic children employ these movement behaviors for providing sensory stimulation, expression to avoid demands, making a request or drawing attention or as anxiolytic.

Screening: Easy and convenient method applied to asses a child's typical growth and development. Screening tools are simple approaches that identify children who are at risk for developmental delay disorders from the normal ones.

Scripting: Echolalia is sometimes referred to as scripting which involves repetition of words, phrases, intonation or sounds of speech of others or from movies or from favorite books.

Self-Stimulating Behavior: refer to behavioral repetitive movement patterns or body positions such as hand flapping or body rocking. Autistic children employ these movement behaviors for providing sensory stimulation, expression to avoid demands, making a request or drawing attention or as anxiolytic. Sometimes it can involve objects such as tossing string in air.

Sensory Development: Refers to the capacity of children to detect and respond appropriately to both internal (Temperature) and external (smell) sensory input. This ability develops at different stages of the growth.

Sensory Stimulation: Children with ASD often display odd behaviors such as toe walking or finger flicking which can be related to anxiety, tactile defensiveness or self-stimulatory. These behavioral mannerisms may have significance to the child by providing sensory stimulation or communicating to avoid demands or request a desired object or attention or soothing when anxious.

Shared Attention: it is the tendency of children to share attention with their caregiver during their first year of life. Infants at an early stage normally learn to seek joint attention by shifting gaze between an object of interest and the caregiver and back to the object, following the gaze of others and using gestures to attract others attention to objects.

Social Reciprocity: Refers to oscillatory flow of social interaction. It demonstrates how the behavior of one person affects and is affected by the behavior of another person and vice versa.

Speech impediment: It is a form expression disorder where normal speech is disrupted. The speech disruption can be in the form of stammering, lisp, stuttering or mis-articulation of certain words or sounds.

Spoken Language: It is the

application of verbal behavior or speech to communicate or express thoughts, ideas and feelings with others.

Symbolic Play: Refers to ability or capacity of children to pretend to perform certain tasks and to be something or someone else.

Tantrum: Refers to expression of intense emotions or immediate frustration during developmental process of children normally occurring when a child is unable to express their emotions and feelings due to deficient verbal skills.

Verbal Signs: Refers to the use of speech or spoken words to pass or exchange information, ideas or thoughts to other people. It employs use of appropriate sounds, stress and different tones to express spoken words to convey the intended message.

Words: Refers to speech, sounds or words that is identifiable and has specific meaning that can be understood by the intended audience or recipient.

Made in the USA
Middletown, DE
18 October 2020